One Leaf Rides the Wind

For Bruce, my partner on the path,
and our blossoms, Alyssa and Samantha.
Heartfelt thanks to Jill and Kendra, Nadine,
Sandy, and Joan—gardeners all!
—C.D.M.

For Hannah
—S.K.H.

One Leaf Rides the Wind
COUNTING IN A JAPANESE GARDEN

by Celeste Davidson Mannis

pictures by Susan Kathleen Hartung

PUFFIN BOOKS

1

One leaf rides the wind.
Quick as I am, it's quicker!
Just beyond my grasp.

Within the burnished depths of an autumn leaf
is the story of seasons past and seasons yet to come.

2

Two carved temple dogs
snarling over my shoulder.
Sit! Guard the garden.

Long ago, Buddhist monks trained shih tzu dogs to
guard their temples. Today, temple dog statues flank the
entrances of gardens and temples, talismans against
disasters such as fire, flood, and earthquake.

Suddenly I'm tall!
A miniature forest —
three pots on a wall.

Bonsai is the art of growing trees in pots or trays.
Through careful trimming and wiring, the beauty of a full-grown tree is recreated in miniature. Often called "heaven and earth in one container" bonsai celebrates the harmony possible between man and nature.

4

From eaves to blue skies,
four startled birds take flight. Shoo!
A cat prowls the roof.

Shinto, the native religion of Japan, teaches respect for
nature in its many and varied forms. Kami are spirits
believed to dwell in all natural things. Animals, plants,
rocks, water, and the sky are homes for these spirits.

5

Smiling pagoda.
Five roofs stretch to the heavens.
We shelter beneath.

The gently upturned roofs of the pagoda stand for earth,
water, fire, wind, and sky. With its soaring silhouette,
the pagoda is a prominent feature of the garden,
and a favorite place to pray or meditate.

6

Outside the teahouse,
six wooden sandals gathered
neatly in a row.

Before entering the teahouse guests place their shoes
on the *kutsunugi-ishi*, or "shoe receiving stone."
Shoes are removed before entering the teahouse,
to honor the purity of the tea ceremony.

7

On a lacquered tray
seven sweet surprises lie.
Hungry tummies growl.

Every movement and gesture of the tea ceremony reflects
the principles of harmony, respect, purity, and tranquility.
The tea master prepares frothy green tea and a simple meal.
Sweet cakes made from rice, soybean paste, or pureed
chestnuts are molded into the shapes of seasonal flowers,
fruits, and leaves and served after the meal.

8

What do flowers dream?
Adrift on eight pond pillows,
pink-cheeked blossoms rest.

White, yellow, and pink lotus flowers flourish in ponds,
their plump blossoms perched atop floating leaves, or pads.
They represent purity and mirror the soul's ability to reach
beyond muddy waters to the sunlight of a better existence.

9

Hoping for some crumbs,
they nibble at my fingers.
Nine glittering koi.

Koi fish are admired for their colorful appearance and
hardiness. They are also a popular symbol of
determination and strength. Ancient legend tells of a koi
fish that struggled up a huge waterfall in order to be
transformed into a dragon.

10

Ten lanterns waiting.
When darkness falls they sparkle,
pleased to light the way.

Delicately carved stone lanterns are displayed
throughout the garden. In the evening
their twinkling light helps guide visitors,
illuminating a branch here, a bit of path there....

One leaf rides the wind.
Quick as it is, I'm quicker!
I reach for the sky.

The Japanese garden is a restful place, removed from the cares and worries of everyday life. It is a world that offers hope of harmony between people, nature, and the heavens. The garden encourages visitors to look inward and find that world of peace and tranquility within themselves.

Haiku is a form of poetry that originated in Japan many hundreds of years ago. The poems are very brief, often recited in a single breath. Spare style and snapshot-like images of nature stimulate the senses and challenge the reader to make connections between the natural world and the nature of man.

Haiku was originally written in a three-line format, with each line having five, seven, and five syllables, respectively. That convention is no longer strictly followed, as haiku is now enjoyed in many different languages, each with its own unique set of characteristics.

PUFFIN BOOKS
Published by Penguin Group
Penguin Young Readers Group,
345 Hudson Street, New York, New York 10014, U.S.A.
Penguin Books Ltd, 80 Strand, London WC2R ORL, England
Penguin Books Australia Ltd, 250 Camberwell Road, Camberwell, Victoria 3124, Australia
Penguin Books Canada Ltd, 10 Alcorn Avenue, Toronto, Ontario, Canada M4V 3B2
Penguin Group (NZ), cnr Airborne and Rosedale Roads, Albany, Auckland 1310, New Zealand

First published in the United States of America by Viking,
a division of Penguin Putnam Books for Young Readers, 2002
Published by Puffin Books, a division of Penguin Young Readers Group, 2005

19 20 18

THE LIBRARY OF CONGRESS HAS CATALOGED THE VIKING EDITION AS FOLLOWS:
Mannis, Celeste D.
One leaf rides the wind: counting in a Japanese garden / by Celeste D. Mannis ;
illustrated by Susan Hartung
p. cm.
Summary: In this collection of haiku poems, a young girl walks through a Japanese garden and discovers
many delights, from one leaf to ten stone lanterns. Includes notes about Japanese religion and philosophy.
ISBN: 0-670-03524 (hc)
1. Gardens, Japanese—Juvenile poetry. 2. Children's poetry, American. 3. Nature—Juvenile poetry.
4. Counting-out rhymes. 5. Haiku, American.
[1. Gardens, Japanese—Poetry. 2. Nature—Poetry. 3. Haiku. 4. American poetry. 5. Counting.]
I. Hartung, Susan Kathleen, ill. II. Title.
PS3613.A3625 O54 2002 [E]—dc21 2002001024

Puffin Books ISBN 978-0-14-240195-8

Printed in the United States of America
Set in Cochin
Book design by Teresa Kietlinski

The illustrations for this book were created using oil paint glazes on sealed paper.
The paint is blotted and manipulated to create the different effects.